MARTIAL ARTS IN ACTION

AIKIDO

MARTIAL ARTS IN ACTION
AIKIDO

BY RUTH BJORKLUND

Marshall Cavendish Benchmark
New York

For Lily, Owen, and Sensei Chris

Published by Marshall Cavendish Benchmark
An imprint of Marshall Cavendish Corporation

Other Marshall Cavendish Offices:
Marshall Cavendish International (Asia) Private Limited, 1 New Industrial Road, Singapore
536196 • Marshall Cavendish International (Thailand) Co Ltd. 253 Asoke, 12th Flr, Sukhumvit
21 Road, Klongtoey Nua, Wattana, Bangkok 10110, Thailand • Marshall Cavendish (Malaysia)
Sdn Bhd, Times Subang, Lot 46, Subang Hi-Tech Industrial Park, Batu Tiga, 40000 Shah Alam,
Selangor Darul Ehsan, Malaysia

Marshall Cavendish is a trademark of Times Publishing Limited

All websites were available and accurate when this book was sent to press.

Library of Congress Cataloging-in-Publication Data

Bjorklund, Ruth.
Aikido / Ruth Bjorklund.
p. cm. — (Martial arts in action)
Includes index.
ISBN 978-0-7614-4931-7 (print)
ISBN 978-1-60870-361-6 (ebook)
1. Aikido—Juvenile literature.
2. Martial arts for children—Juvenile
literature. I. Title.
GV1114.35.B55 2012
796.815'4—dc22
2010013820

Editor: Peter Mavrikis
Publisher: Michelle Bisson
Art Director: Anahid Hamparian
Series design by Kristen Branch

Photo Research by Candlepants Incorporated

Cover Photo: © Jean-Yves Ruszniewski/TempSport/Corbis

The photographs in this book are used by permission and through the courtesy of:
Alamy Images: © Megapress, 2, 33; © Steve Skjold, 6; © Roberto Pastrovicchio, 12,
24, 32, 41; © JTB Photo Communications, Inc., 16; © Milestone Media, 22; © Pat Behnke,
23; © Eliane Sulle, 42; © Photo Japan, 43. © 2010 *www.robertburkhalter.com*, 8, 10,
11, 26, 27, 30, 34, 36, 38, 39. *Getty Images*, 19; DAJ, 21. *Shutterstock*, 28.

Printed in Malaysia
1 3 5 6 4 2

CONTENTS

CHAPTER ONE

AN AIKIDOKA

"**I MOVE DIFFERENTLY THAN ANYONE I KNOW,**" says Owen, an *aikidoka*, or someone who practices aikido. He says that he has practiced aikido for six years and it has changed his life. "I have learned to be tough, but loose, like a rubber band," he explains. "You could say that I go with the flow, but really, I control the flow!" In aikido, students learn special ways to roll and fall, called *ukemi waza*.

Owen says that in school classmates are always asking, "What would you do if I did this to you?" Owen says he would show them his best choice, but would never act on it, because if they did not have the right training, he could easily hurt them. But sometimes practicing aikido does hurt a little, says Owen. "It's never been

THE FIRST IMPORTANT LESSON AN AIKIDOKA MUST LEARN IS HOW TO FALL SAFELY.

TWO STUDENTS BEGIN THEIR PRACTICE WITH BASIC MOVES SUCH AS WRIST TURNS AND JOINT LOCKS.

serious, but I have felt pain." Another reason Owen does not like to show others what he can do is that he does not want them to think that because he has shown them a move, they know how to do it. "I don't want them to try things on other people!"

Owen's instructor, or **sensei**, thinks young people should study aikido in an aikido school. "Aikido teaches how to coordinate mind and body, how to build self-confidence, and how to get along with others. It tells you to say to yourself, 'I am somebody.'" He adds that aikido is very moral, that it teaches students to respect each other, as well as themselves. Aikidoka learn to be very aware of each other. Aikido is the only martial art that truly requires two people—their paired practice is called *kumi waza*. Even if a person practices alone, he or she practices with an "invisible" partner, which is called *hitori waza*. The key to aikido practice is for partners to blend their energies. Being especially aware of each other and each other's likely movements is called *zanshin*.

Although akidoka train for "ultimate life and death conflict," Owen's sensei says that people can use what they learn in aikido to manage small daily conflicts. Most daily conflicts, he says, are verbal. "For example, when I am insulted or verbally attacked, I just turn away. I try never to argue or manipulate. I want to negotiate something agreeable to everyone. I let the other person say everything he or she wants to say and I just wait for my turn to speak." Owen agrees that aikido has taught him to be patient and understanding with his friends, family, classmates, teachers, and others. But he does not just give in. Instead, he speaks up and tries to find a common solution. If he cannot, then he does not let it bother him. He says, "I

AN AIKIDO STUDENT LEARNS A WRIST LOCK, AN EFFECTIVE WAY TO RESTRAIN OR CONTROL AN OPPONENT.

know how to talk about things without putting people on the spot and when they try to put me on the spot, I have learned how to be calm and let things go." His sensei agrees and adds that the best way to get along with others is to avoid situations that can lead to trouble in the first place. But if trouble happens, his sensei says, "Aikido is not about attacking or hurting someone but about defending yourself and neutralizing the attack."

Owen's sensei explains that there are different styles of aikido. Some can be very military, while others are very gentle. Some

STUDENTS OF DIFFERENT AGES AND EXPERIENCE LEVELS OFTEN PRACTICE TOGETHER.

aikidoka are so peaceful that their practice is almost like yoga. "As a matter of fact," says sensei, "Owen helps me with a class I teach for young people with disabilities. In that class we focus on the yoga-like qualities of aikido. The kids learn core strength and balance. Because they have to practice together, they also develop better social skills, like we all do."

On the other hand, some aikido styles are more aggressive. When aikido was being developed as a martial art, one original sensei was a samurai, a Japanese swordsman. He was very military in his practice.

Owen practices aikido with a sword called a **bokken**. Many might wonder why a peaceful martial art such as aikido includes sword

STUDENTS TRAIN WITH A WOODEN SWORD, CALLED A BOKKEN, BEFORE USING A METAL BLADE, OR KATANA.

handling. "It's about real life," says Owen. "There is no arguing with a big piece of metal. Either you find an opening and go for it, or if you see that there isn't one, then you get out of the way. What you learn is that you don't block, you parry." Aikido is really about harmony and movement with others. It is not about destruction or competition. "That's why Hollywood doesn't make aikido movies!" Owen says with a grin.

CHAPTER TWO

THE HISTORY OF AIKIDO

"**THE SECRET OF AIKIDO** is to make yourself become one with the universe and to go along with its natural movements. One who has attained this secret holds the universe in him or herself and can say, 'I am the universe,'" so wrote Morihei Ueshiba (pronounced More-ah-hi You-sheeba), the founder of aikido. Aikido is a modern Japanese form of **budu**, or martial art. The word, broken down, means: *ai*=harmony, *ki*=spiritual energy, and *do*=the path.

Morihei Ueshiba was born on December 14, 1883, in Tanabe, Japan, a small mountain village. He was the only son of four children. His father was a community leader and his mother was an educated woman and a devout Buddhist who loved literature, practiced calligraphy, and painted. Morihei was a small and rather

THE FOUNDER OF AIKIDO, MORIHEI UESHIBA, WAS DECLARED A SACRED NATIONAL TREASURE OF JAPAN.

weak child, but by virtue of being the only son, it was expected that he accompany his father on pilgrimages to Buddhist shrines and help him carry heavy bags of rice and other goods up to their mountain home. His parents each wanted a meaningful future for their son, though they differed on what that should be. Morihei's mother hoped that he would become a Buddhist monk, and he attended a monastery school. But his father, a man whose forebears had been samurai warriors, rejected the idea. He encouraged Morihei to develop strength by swimming, sumo wrestling, and sword handling.

MOUNT KOYA, HOME TO MANY SHRINES AND TEMPLES, RISES FROM THE SEA NEAR TANABE, JAPAN, THE BIRTHPLACE OF MORIHEI UESHIBA.

Ultimately, Morihei learned from both of his parents. He grew up strong and healthy, with a deep respect for nature, art, and religion.

Morihei proved to be an able and quick-witted student, and after finishing school he left Tanabe and started a small business. As he became more successful, with more employees, he had more time to study sword handling and jujutsu, a form of martial art now often called jujitsu. But after a few years, he fell ill, and was forced to sell his business and move back home with his parents.

They nurtured him back to health and by 1904, Morihei decided to join the military. War had broken out between Japan and Russia, and Morihei wanted to follow in the path of his warrior ancestors. Unfortunately, the army refused him because he was under 5 feet (1.5 meters) tall, too short to meet the minimum height requirement. At first angry, Morihei resolved to find a way to enlist. He focused on strengthening his body and perfecting his knowledge of swordsmanship. He even hung from trees in the forest, in the hopes of stretching his body. On his second attempt, Morihei was accepted into the army reserves. He was certified to teach swordsmanship and as a teacher, became very valuable to his unit. But Morihei continually requested to be allowed to fight in actual combat, and at last his commanding officers relented.

On the battlefield, Morihei stunned his fellow soldiers by running to the front lines and dodging oncoming bullets. He seemed to possess an extrasensory awareness that allowed him to see the bullets as streaks of light and be able to avoid them. In hand-to-hand combat, Morihei studied his opponents' moves, and, in the face of their aggression, he remained calm. Using their own energy against them, Morihei deflected his enemies' advances and defeated them resoundingly. For his bravery and remarkable battlefield accomplishments, he became known as the "soldier god."

After the war, Morihei's father asked him to return to Tanabe. His father built him a small *dojo*, or practice studio, and invited a traveling jujitsu master to instruct Morihei on the finer points of budu. Morihei studied jujitsu with the master along with judo, swordsmanship, and spear fighting. Morihei's strength and his state of mind improved so much that living at home with his parents no longer disturbed him.

In 1912, the Japanese government was concerned about overpopulation and urged people to spread out into remote, undeveloped areas. Morihei eagerly chose to lead fifty-four families into the wilderness. They settled on Japan's northernmost island, Hokkaido. The first winter was harsh and bone-chillingly cold. The villagers were unprepared and many died. But Morihei led those who persevered as they built homes and towns and established farms, ranches, and lumber mills. He was a born teacher and leader and in this role as Hokkaido's mentor, Morihei blossomed into a hard-working man with patience, intuitiveness, kindness, and a sense of purpose.

In Hokkaido, Morihei sought out other budu masters and religious thinkers. One was Sokaku Takeda, a master who practiced a 1,000-year-old form of jujitsu, handed down through generations of his family. Though Takeda was not as tall nor as strong as Morihei, he defeated him in every contest. Morihei said that Takedo showed him the true essence of budu.

MORIHEI UESHIBA'S BATTLEFIELD EXPERIENCE TAUGHT HIM TO UNDERSTAND THAT A PERSON SHOULD ALWAYS BE PREPARED FOR AN ATTACK TO ANY PART OF THE BODY FROM ANY DIRECTION.

THE GREAT TEACHER

There are two principals behind aikido, one is a spiritual and physical unity, and the other is peaceful and social unity. Morihei studied **Shinto**, an ancient religion that sees holiness in all things. Followers of Shinto believe that all creatures and plants are gods and that nature should be worshiped. Besides worshiping at shrines and temples, followers of Shinto worship mountains, rivers, rocks, seas, stars, and planets. While studying Shintoism, Takedo visited Morihei and they spent several weeks working together. Takedo certified Morihei as a teacher, or sensei. Through many influences, Morihei saw that his new martial art, which at that time he called *aiki bujutsu,* had become an expression of Shintoism and a "living prayer for world health, harmony, and prosperity."

Word began to spread about Morihei, now called Ueshiba-sensei. In 1920, he moved with his family to Kyoto, Japan, and opened a school. Many came to visit him and when other senseis practiced with him, Ueshiba-sensei bested them all. In 1927, a high-ranking naval officer took notice of Ueshiba-sensei and invited him to open a dojo in Tokyo. He accepted, and soon taught students from all over Japan. People began to refer to him as **O'Sensei**, meaning "great teacher."

O'Sensei was committed to the principle that aikido, now called *aiki budu,* was not a method of fighting but a spiritual practice. In 1941, Japan went to war with the United States and its allies. Saddened by the war, O'Sensei left Tokyo and moved to a farm to think and pray. At the end of the war, Japan had an occupied

MORIHEI UESHIBA TRAVELED OFTEN IN THE MOUNTAINS STOPPING AND PRAYING AT ANCIENT SACRED SITES, SUCH AS THIS BUDDHIST TEMPLE.

government which forbade the practice of martial arts. Three years later, when the ban was lifted, the government licensed *aiki budu* under the name aikido and O'Sensei's son became the master of his Tokyo dojo.

Today, that Tokyo dojo is the world headquarters of the Aikido Foundation. O'Sensei himself taught and practiced until his death at age eighty-six. His gift to the world is a form of martial art that is about peace and not about force and competition. As O'Sensei wrote, "Aikido is not about defeating one's enemy. It is the way to unite human beings and guide the world toward harmony."

TO SHOW RESPECT FOR O'SENSEI, AKIDOKAS BOW TOWARD THE ALTAR (SHOMEN) EACH TIME THEY ENTER OR LEAVE THE DOJO.

AIKIDO IN THE WORLD

Aikido started out as the result of a series of events experienced by a young man from a small Japanese village, and has today become one of the world's most thoughtful and graceful martial art forms. In 1951, an aikido master introduced the practice of aikido to students in France, and two years later, the United States. Presently, the International Aikido Foundation has members in forty-three countries including Finland, Mexico, Paraguay, Serbia, South Africa, Lebanon, and New Zealand. Followers the world over recognize that O'Sensei's teachings are as meaningful now as ever before.

MANY AKIDOKA PREFER TRAINING OUTDOORS, ESPECIALLY WHEN PRACTICING WITH WEAPONS.

IN THE DOJO

AIKIDO IS A MARTIAL ART that is grounded in peace, harmony, and respect for living things. Aikidoka should always be polite and honor their dojo. Aikido dojos have an altar-like area on the wall called a *shomen*, where paintings and photographs, especially photographs of O'Sensei, are hung. Whenever entering or leaving the dojo, aikidoka bow toward the shomen. It is expected that everyone show respect for each other as well as their dojo and their practice. Before beginning, students bow to their sensei and he or she will bow in return. Before performing with a partner, aikidoka also bow to one another.

TO FALL SAFELY, AN AIKIDOKA MUST REMEMBER TO TUCK IN THE CHIN, EXHALE WHEN HITTING THE GROUND, AND MOST IMPORTANTLY, TO STAY RELAXED.

To prepare for aikido class, aikidoka remove their shoes and make sure that they have arrived clean and neat, with hair tied back, no jewelry, and only simple, comfortable clothing underneath their aikido uniform, called a *gi*. The gi is a medium weight white jacket with a belt and a pair of loose white pants. Most aikido belts are white (*kyu* in Japanese), although senior aikidoka and senseis may wear black (*dan*) belts. In some studios in the United States, there are a series of belt colors that reflect achievement levels, but that is not traditional, as aikido is about non-competitiveness. Many senseis and expert akidoka also wear a large, black, open-sided skirt over their gi called a *hakama*.

A CLASS KNEELS IN THE SEIZA POSITION WHILE THE SENSEI SPEAKS.

Once everyone has arrived and bowed towards the shomen, they take a kneeling position on the mat in a position known as *seiza* (say-zah). Aikidoka kneel in seiza in the beginning and at the end of each class, or when their sensei is speaking. They also bow from seiza position by placing their hands in front of them and bending their heads to the floor.

Once practice starts, aikidoka stand and position themselves into a basic aikido stance. Unlike other martial arts, aikido has only one basic stance, called a *hanmi*. In hanmi, the aikidoka stands straight upright and steps forward with either the right or left foot. The back foot turns slightly out and the heel of the forward foot is in line with the middle of the back foot. With hands, feet, and hips centered the body forms a triangle, which gives the body stability and the ability to move freely. It is important for maximum strength and balance to be centered, that is, to focus on the area just below the navel. Special exercises and breathing techniques help strengthen the body's center core.

IN THE HANMI POSITION, AKIDOKA CENTER THEIR BODY IN A TRIANGLE SHAPE. PERFECTING THIS STANCE MAKES THE BODY NEARLY IMMOVEABLE.

How to Tie an Obi

An obi is the fabric belt that holds the jacket of the gi securely in place. The knot should be flat and diamond shaped. When first learning how to tie the obi, it is often helpful to "tag" one of the ends. Many obis have a small label stitched to the end of one side. If there is no label, "tag" it by making a small mark with thread or pencil that can be removed later. To help understand these directions, one end will be called the tag end and the other will be called the blank end.

- Hold the center of the obi in front of you so that the hanging ends are of equal length.
- Let the tag end be on your left side.
- Take the center of the obi and hold it against the middle of your stomach.
- Take each end and wrap them in opposite directions around your waist.
- When the ends meet at the center of your back, cross the blank end in your right hand over the tag end in your left hand.
- Once crossed, tuck the tag end under the belt and pull each end forward.
- The tag end is now in your right hand, the blank end in your left.

THE FINAL TIE OF AN OBI SHOULD RESEMBLE AN ARROW POINTING TO THE LEFT.

- Cross the blank end over the tag end.
- Turn the blank end in toward you and tuck it up under the belt.
- Now turn the blank end down over the belt and cross it over the tag end, forming an opening.
- With your left hand, hold where the ends cross.
- With your right hand, pull the tag end (now underneath) up and over the blank end and down into the opening.
- Now take an end in each hand and pull outwards horizontally.
- Your obi knot is now secure and will not get in the way of your practice.

MOVING OUT OF THE WAY

Aikido is a non-violent martial art. Practitioners do not kick or punch, but instead grasp, fend off, roll away from, or throw their partner using the partner's own energy. O'Sensei said that the mainstay of aikido technique is about gracefully getting out of the way. The techniques of aikido include learning how to use circular motions to

IN THE STANCE CALLED AI-HANMI, PARTNERS FACE EACH OTHER WITH THE SAME FOOT FORWARD.

deflect opponents, how to turn and stride, as well as many types of throwing, falling, and rolling. When one partner charges forward, the other averts the attack by using various circular movements with his or her arms and legs to thwart the partner's advances. The aikidoka does not block the partner but rather uses the partner's own forward motion to redirect it. After controlling the partner's movement, the aikidoka may restrain him or her using wrist grasps, joint locks, and unbalancing techniques. In their encounter, the aikidoka combine their energies and move together in flowing movements, demonstrating the essential aikido principle of harmony.

The strength of aikido movements comes from being non-resistant. Some compare aikido to being like a flexible willow tree that bends in the wind but does not break as would an inflexible oak tree. There are three types of non-resistant techniques: blending, leading, and controlling. Leading guides a partner's advances beyond where they intended to go and puts him or her off balance. Blending means combining one another's energies and moving with the attack, and controlling means being centered and striding toward the partner's attack.

WEAPONRY

O'Sensei was a master swordsman and so he incorporated weapons into aikido. Many aikidoka use wooden training weapons such as a sword called a *bokken,* a knife called a **tanto**, and a **jo**, which is a short staff. Experienced aikidoka may use a **katana**, which is an ancient sword used by samurais. Although weapons are used in aikido, they are not as necessary as they are in other forms of martial arts.

ALMOST ALL AIKIDO TECHNIQUES CAN BE DONE WHILE KNEELING, INCLUDING PRACTICE WITH A SWORD OR KNIFE.

MAKING THE CHOICE

Learning to perform aikido is a commitment of time, energy, and a focused mind. Beginners first learn stretching and breathing exercises as well as basic positions and movements. Often getting to that point can take up to a year. Frequent practice is the real key to success.

Aikido is a non-violent, peaceful, and spiritual martial art. It is not for everyone. Some people chose other martial arts for their more aggressive forms of fighting. Aikido is not a martial art that trains people in self defense outside of the dojo, yet it does provide many desirable advantages, such as physical fitness, strength, balance, agility, and self confidence. Aikido is beautiful to watch and uplifting to perform. Each time O'Sensei began a performance he chanted, *Oom Oomuu*, which means, "Let the dance of the gods begin!"

PROTECTING YOURSELF

AN AKIDOKA DEFLECTS A BLOW FROM HIS PARTNER, PUTTING HIM OFF BALANCE.

If you are studying a martial art in order to protect yourself from an attacker in the world outside of the dojo, aikido is not the ideal sport. Yet aikido provides excellent conditioning that can still come to your aid.

First of all, students of aikido learn to distract and to get out of the way. When confronted by an attacker, aikidoka can react efficiently and with a degree of calm. They have also developed physical fitness that helps them quickly flee from an attack. Everyone hopes to avoid danger by staying away from questionable areas and trying to avoid confrontations. But aikidoka have many advantages, they know how to remain calm and to react to others with respect and kindness whenever possible.

When exiting from the confrontation, or when calm discussion does not work, very experienced aikidoka may use some basic moves that can be effective in fending off or escaping an attack. The most common method is to use *atemi*, which is a sudden strategic poke or slap to a vital area such as the eye or under the chin. If this strike is done at the right moment, it will distract the attacker long enough to flee. Instructors warn that if an aikidoka strikes with an atemi move too early, it can be the aikidoka who is accused of being the attacker.

How to Choose A Dojo

There may be several local dojos, or just one or two. It is best to visit any dojo you are interested in joining before committing. When visiting the dojo read all the brochures and other information (such as bulletin boards) that are available. Even if there is only one dojo in the area, it is still important to observe a class and make an appointment with the instructor.

STUDENTS IN THIS DOJO ARE PRACTICING WARM UP EXERCISES.

Feel free to ask him or her questions. Here are some thoughts to consider:

- Is there information about etiquette? (Some senseis are very formal, others less so.)
- Does the instructor have a certain emphasis (such as weaponry or O'Sensei's Shinto / Buddhist philosophy)?
- Is there a good fit with class times and your schedule?
- Are there classes at beginners' level? How many students are in each class?
- What are practice expectations?
- Do you attend tournaments? How often and how far do you travel?
- Are there periods when the dojo is available for practice outside of class time?

For help in finding a nearby aikido dojo, you can contact the United States Aikido Federation or other local organizations.

CHAPTER FOUR

AIKIDO IN EVERYDAY LIFE

LEARNING AIKIDO AND UNDERSTANDING the basic principles can have a positive influence on everyday life. By taking O'Sensei's beliefs in non-violence and harmony to heart, people who follow the ways of aikido learn to avoid confrontations and reduce feelings of anger and stress. When problems do come up, akidoka can face conflict calmly and with respect for others. O'Sensei told his followers that "I do not think badly of others when they treat me unkindly. Rather, I feel gratitude towards them for giving me the opportunity to train myself to handle adversity."

Aikido teaches people how to be sensitive to others' actions and emotions, as well as being aware of their own. Careful watching and waiting during aikido practice and demonstrations helps develop

STUDENTS OF AIKIDO LEARN COOPERATION AND RESPECT FOR EACH OTHER.

AKIDOKA ARE NOT COMPETITIVE OR VIOLENT AND SHARE A PHILOSOPHY OF NOT HURTING ANYONE.

students' concentration skills so that they can focus better in school and learn how to do new activities quicker, such as a job, sports, or games. One of the hardest things to do in life is to face difficult situations directly, such as getting untangled from an argument with a friend or explaining a missing assignment to a parent or teacher. The best outcomes take place by being honest and open. Similarly, in practice, akidoka learn to face an opponent head-on by stepping toward the attack with their whole body and mind. This is called

BEING SUCCESSFUL IN AIKIDO DOES NOT DEPEND ON STRENGTH OR SIZE.

irimi and aikidoka who learn to be comfortable with irimi are better able to face others eye to eye.

During practice and demonstrations, aikidoka hope to achieve a goal called **mushin**, which means "no-mind." Mushin is not unlike what athletes describe as "being in the zone." In other words, it is about skillfully performing an action or challenge without thinking about it. Once aikidoka become used to the feeling of mushin, they can carry it over to other parts of their lives, such as in school, sports, or creative activities.

DEFENSE TECHNIQUES

Aikido has thousands of different techniques. There are two basic categories and seven basic defense techniques. The categories are controlling and throwing. The defense techniques include:

- *Atemi*—Vital point striking. In some martial arts, atemi is a strike to a sensitive area meant to cause pain. But an aikidoka will make a quick, darting finger poke at a vital area, such as eyes or under the chin, in order to distract.

- *Tai sabaki*—Simple body-shifting movements. Tai sabaki is used from the very beginning of a demonstration and relies on the aikidoka being centered and able respond automatically to an opponent's unexpected movements.

- *Nage waza*—Defensive moves that attempt to blend a partner's energy.

- *Katame*—The first step toward a throw. The aikidoka locks the wrist of the opponent in order to control the shoulder and complete the throw.

- *Irimi*—A movement toward the partner with the intention of throwing.
- *Rofuse*—The act of throwing the opponent by using pressure to his or her joints.
- *Kansetu*—Stopping or immobilizing a partner by using joint restraints such as grasping the wrist and upper arm in order to set the partner off balance.

PRACTICING WITH TWO OPPONENTS, THE AKIDOKA HAS USED SPEEDED UP MOVEMENTS TO FEND THE OPPONENTS OFF ONE BY ONE.

THE BENEFITS OF AIKIDO

Aikido is a martial art that can benefit anyone. People of any size, shape, or age can be successful, and frequent practice always leads to a healthier, stronger, and more coordinated body. Girls and boys and men and women can all practice the art of aikido—mature, strong muscles not being as important as balance, coordination, and focus. Adults are often interested in aikido philosophy and the teachings of O'Sensei, while young people especially enjoy learning the movements such as rolling, falling, and flipping. In adult classes, the instructors generally do more talking and explaining, and in young people's classes instructors mostly teach by example, showing students how to roll, throw, and control. When young students advance to higher levels, very often they choose to remain

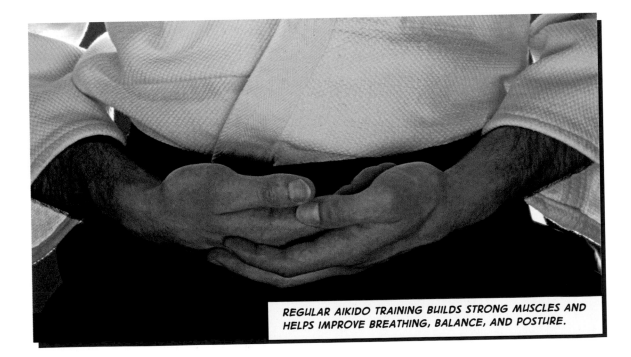

REGULAR AIKIDO TRAINING BUILDS STRONG MUSCLES AND HELPS IMPROVE BREATHING, BALANCE, AND POSTURE.

THIS AIKIDO DEMONSTRATION IS A "FRIENDLY" COMPETITION WHERE PERFORMERS ARE GRADED ON STYLE, TECHNIQUE, BALANCE, AND THE ABILITY TO FLOW WITH A PARTNER'S ENERGY.

with people their own age rather than joining adult classes. But for any student, aikido can be both fun and meaningful.

In aikido, the emphasis is on interaction between people and not combativeness. It is about solving conflict or aggression peacefully. Classmates usually have a different partner for each class or sometimes switch partners during a single class. In tournaments, there are always several opponents. Students of aikido are likely to have a strong sense of teamwork and improved social skills because aikido requires that they combine their energies and move together. Aikidoka say that performing in front of other people at tournaments helps them overcome their shyness in other social situations. Most importantly, aikido helps people feel pride, confidence, and a sense of accomplishment, leading them to better relationships and physical fitness and more enjoyment and success in daily life.

GLOSSARY

aikidoka—A person or persons who practice aikido (singular and plural).

atemi—A strike or poke to a partner's vital area such as eyes, groin, or under the chin.

bokken—An aikido practice sword.

budu—Japanese word for martial art.

dojo—A martial art practice studio.

gi—An aikido "uniform," consisting of loose jacket, belt, and pants.

hakama—A loose open sided black skirt worn by senseis and senior aikidoka.

hanmi—The basic aikido stance.

hitori waza—Aikido practice with an "invisible" partner.

irimi—The act of entering into an attack.

jo—Wooden training staff.

katana—Sword used by Japanese samurai warriors.

kumi waza—The act of practicing aikido with a partner.

mushin—Japanese word to describe performing actions skillfully without having to think about them.

O'Sensei—Honorific used to refer to Morihei Ueshiba.

obi—Fabric belt worn over gi.

seiza—Kneeling position.

sensei—Japanese word for instructor or teacher.

Shinto—Ancient Japanese religion.

shomen—Altar-like area of dojo.

tanto—Wooden practice knife.

ukemi waza—Rolling and falling techniques.

zanshin—Being aware of others, one's surroundings, and one's self.

FIND OUT MORE

BOOKS

Randall, Pamela. *Aikido*. New York : PowerKids Press, 2003.

Robertson, Lauren. *The Best Book of Martial Arts*. New York: Kingfisher, 2005.

Scandiffio, Laura. *The Martial Arts Book*. Toronto: Annick Press, 2003.

WEBSITES

Aikido International
http://aikido-international.org

Aikido West Beginner's Handbook
http://www.aikido-west.org/handbook/index.html

O'Sensei's Last Performance
http://www.youtube.com/watch?v=XoDK3XuvZWw

The United States Aikido Federation
http://www.usaikifed.com

INDEX

Page numbers in **boldface** are illustrations.

ABOUT THE AUTHOR

Ruth Bjorklund lives on Bainbridge Island, a ferry ride away from Seattle, Washington. Her daughter, Lily, has practiced aikido for several years. Both Lily and her sensei were excited to help provide information and insight for the writing of this book.